Digital Real Estate 101

A Comprehensive Guide to Investing and Thriving in the Online Property Market

DIGITAL REAL ESTATE 101

First edition. October 31, 2023.

ISBN: 979-8223420590

Written by Andan Maharma.

Adnan Maharma

Chapter Outline:

The Rise of Digital Real Estate
    1.1 Understanding the Concept of Digital Real Estate
    1.2 The Evolution of Online Properties
    1.3 Benefits and Opportunities in the Digital Real Estate Market

Part I: Building a Foundation in Digital Real Estate

2. Types of Digital Properties
   2.1 Websites and Domains
   2.2 Social Media Assets
   2.3 Virtual Real Estate and Metaverses
   Researching and Evaluating Digital Properties
   3.1 Market Analysis and Trends
   3.2 Assessing the Potential Value of Online Properties
   3.3 Due Diligence and Risk Assessment

Monetization Strategies for Digital Properties
   4.1 Advertising and Affiliate Marketing
   4.2 E-commerce and Dropshipping
   4.3 Content Creation and Licensing
   4.4 Virtual Real Estate Rentals and Leasing

Part II: Investing in Digital Real Estate

Part III: Thriving in the Digital Real Estate Market

8. Navigating Legal and Ethical Considerations

Future Trends and Emerging Technologies

Success Stories and Lessons from Digital Real Estate Entrepreneurs

Chapter 1: The Rise of Digital Real Estate

1.1 Understanding the Concept of Digital Real Estate

The concept of real estate has traditionally been associated with physical properties like houses, land, and commercial buildings. However, with the advent of the digital age, a new form of real estate has emerged - digital real estate. Digital real estate refers to virtual properties or online assets that hold value in the digital realm.

Unlike physical real estate, which involves the ownership of tangible assets, digital real estate encompasses a wide range of digital properties such as domain names, websites, social media accounts, mobile applications, and online businesses. These virtual properties have become increasingly valuable and sought after in today's technologically driven world.

Digital real estate holds a unique position in the modern economy. It is intangible, yet its impact is tangible and far-reaching. Companies and individuals are recognizing the power and potential of digital assets to drive business growth, establish brands, and create new revenue streams.

1.2 The Evolution of Online Properties

The evolution of online properties has been closely linked to the growth of the internet and the rapid advancement of digital technologies. In the early days of the internet, digital real estate consisted mainly of domain names. Companies and individuals recognized the importance of securing domain names that matched their brands or represented popular keywords. Domain names became the virtual addresses through which businesses could establish their online presence.

As the internet matured, websites became the primary form of digital real estate. Businesses and individuals started creating websites to establish their online presence, market their products or services, and connect with a global audience. The value of a website depended on factors such as its design, functionality, content, and traffic. Websites became not only informational tools but also platforms for e-commerce, content distribution, and community engagement.

With the rise of social media platforms, online identities and social media accounts also gained significance as forms of digital real estate. Influencers, celebrities, and businesses built large followings on platforms like Instagram, Twitter, and YouTube, turning their profiles into valuable digital assets. Social media platforms provided a new avenue for brand promotion, content creation, and audience engagement, further expanding the realm of digital real estate.

1.3 Benefits and Opportunities in the Digital Real Estate Market

The digital real estate market offers several benefits and exciting opportunities for individuals and businesses alike. One of the key advantages is the global reach and accessibility of online properties. Unlike physical real estate, digital assets can be accessed from anywhere in the world, allowing businesses to expand their customer base beyond geographical boundaries. The internet provides a level playing field, enabling small businesses and startups to compete with larger established entities.

Additionally, digital real estate offers flexibility and scalability. It is easier to modify and update digital properties compared to physical ones. Websites can be redesigned, social media strategies can be adjusted, and online businesses can pivot their offerings with relative ease. This adaptability allows entrepreneurs and marketers to stay agile in a rapidly changing digital landscape. They can experiment with new ideas, iterate on existing concepts, and optimize their digital properties for better performance and customer experience.

Moreover, digital real estate can provide significant returns on investment. Just as physical properties can appreciate in value over time, well-developed and strategically managed online properties can generate substantial income. Websites with high traffic can be monetized through advertising, affiliate marketing, or e-commerce. Social media accounts with a large following can attract brand collaborations and sponsorship deals. Digital real estate offers multiple revenue streams and passive income opportunities, allowing individuals and businesses to diversify their sources of income.

The rise of digital real estate has transformed the way we perceive and capitalize on valuable assets in the digital age. Understanding the concept of digital real estate, recognizing the evolution of online properties, and harnessing the benefits and opportunities in the digital real estate market are essential steps for individuals and businesses looking to thrive in the digital realm. In the following chapters, we will delve deeper into specific aspects of digital real estate, explore successful case studies, and provide practical strategies for maximizing the potential of digital assets. By leveraging the power of digital real estate, individuals and businesses can navigate the digital landscape with confidence, adapt to evolving trends, and unlock new levels of success in the digital realm.

Chapter 2: Types of Digital Properties

2.1 Websites and Domains

Websites and domains are integral components of digital real estate, playing a crucial role in establishing an online presence and driving various business objectives. Let's delve deeper into the world of websites and domains.

A website serves as a virtual representation of a business or individual on the internet. It acts as a platform where information, products, or services are presented to visitors. Websites can be static, containing fixed content, or dynamic, allowing for interactive elements and personalized experiences. The design, functionality, and user experience of a website greatly impact its effectiveness as digital real estate.

When it comes to websites, domain names are of utmost importance. A domain name is the unique web address that users enter into their browsers to access a particular website. It serves as the online identity of a brand or business. Choosing a relevant and memorable domain name is essential for building brand recognition and ensuring easy access for users. It should ideally reflect the business's name, niche, or relevant keywords.

Domain names can be registered through domain registrars, which act as intermediaries between individuals or businesses and the central organization that oversees domain names. Common top-level domains (TLDs) include .com, .org, .net, and country-specific domains like .uk or .de. In recent years, new TLDs have been introduced, offering more specific options like .photography or .store.

The value of a domain name can vary depending on factors such as its length, keyword relevance, branding potential, and market demand. Short, memorable domain names are highly sought after and can command significant prices in the domain marketplace. Some businesses and individuals have even made a profitable business out of buying and selling domains, known as domain flipping.

Websites themselves hold tremendous potential as digital real estate. They serve as virtual storefronts, enabling businesses to reach a global audience and conduct transactions online. A well-designed and user-friendly website can enhance brand credibility, drive traffic, and increase conversions. Websites can generate revenue through various means, including advertising, e-commerce sales, subscriptions, lead generation, or affiliate marketing.

Furthermore, websites are essential for search engine optimization (SEO). By optimizing a website's structure, content, and meta tags, businesses can improve their visibility on search engine result pages, driving organic traffic and potential customers. SEO is a critical aspect of digital marketing and can significantly impact the success of a website as digital real estate.

websites and domains are vital components of digital real estate. Websites act as virtual storefronts, enabling businesses and individuals to showcase their offerings and engage with audiences online. Domain names provide a unique online identity and are essential for establishing brand recognition. Understanding the value and potential of websites and domains is key to leveraging them effectively in the digital realm.

2.2 Social Media Assets

In the realm of digital real estate, social media assets hold significant value and play a crucial role in connecting businesses and individuals with their target audience. Let's explore the world of social media assets and their impact.

Social media assets encompass profiles, pages, and accounts on various social media platforms, such as Facebook, Instagram, Twitter, LinkedIn, YouTube, and more. These platforms have become powerful tools for communication, content sharing, and community building. Social media assets allow businesses and individuals to interact directly with their audience, share updates, and engage in conversations.

Building a strong social media presence involves creating compelling content, developing a consistent brand image, and fostering meaningful connections with followers and fans. By understanding the unique dynamics of each social media platform, businesses and individuals can tailor their content and engagement strategies to maximize their impact.

Social media assets provide numerous benefits in the digital landscape. They allow businesses to reach a vast audience, including potential customers, industry influencers, and brand advocates. Through strategic content creation and community engagement, businesses can establish themselves as authorities in their respective fields and build trust among their followers.

Social media assets also offer opportunities for brand collaborations, influencer partnerships, and sponsorships. Influencers with a substantial following on social media can leverage their assets to collaborate with brands and promote products or services, generating additional revenue streams. Businesses can use their social media assets to showcase their products, share customer testimonials, and run targeted advertising campaigns.

It is important to note that social media assets operate within the platforms' ecosystems, which means they are subject to the platforms' terms of service, algorithms, and policies. Changes in algorithms or policies can significantly impact the reach and visibility of social media content. This highlights the importance of diversifying digital presence by incorporating owned assets like websites and email lists alongside social media assets.

Social media assets can be monetized through various means, including sponsored content, brand partnerships, affiliate marketing, and advertising revenue. Platforms like Instagram and YouTube offer monetization programs that allow content creators to earn revenue based on views, engagement, and ad placements. Businesses can leverage social media assets to drive traffic to their websites, generate leads, and increase conversions.

Building a successful social media presence requires consistency, authenticity, and a deep understanding of the target audience. Regularly posting engaging content, responding to comments and messages, and actively participating in conversations are key elements of effective social media asset management. Analyzing data and insights provided by social media platforms can help businesses refine their strategies and optimize their social media assets for better results.

social media assets have revolutionized the way businesses and individuals connect with their audience. They offer a direct channel for communication, brand promotion, and community engagement. By strategically managing social media assets and leveraging their potential, businesses and individuals can build a strong online presence, amplify their brand message, and tap into new opportunities in the digital realm.

2.3 Virtual Real Estate and Metaverses

In the rapidly evolving landscape of digital real estate, virtual real estate and metaverses have emerged as exciting and transformative concepts. Let's delve into the world of virtual real estate and explore the potential of metaverses.

Virtual real estate refers to the ownership and development of virtual spaces within virtual worlds or online games. These virtual spaces can be bought, sold, and customized by individuals or businesses, much like physical properties in the real world. Virtual real estate allows users to create and curate their own digital environments, opening up a new realm of possibilities.

Virtual worlds and online games, such as Second Life, Minecraft, and Decentraland, provide platforms for users to explore, interact, and build within these virtual spaces. Users can purchase parcels of land, design and construct buildings, and create unique experiences for themselves and others. Virtual real estate has gained traction as a form of digital investment, with users and businesses acquiring virtual properties for various purposes.

Metaverses take the concept of virtual real estate to a whole new level. A metaverse is an immersive digital environment where users can interact with each other and with computer-generated elements. It is a collective virtual space that blends elements of virtual reality, augmented reality, and social networking. Metaverses offer vast opportunities for virtual experiences, social interactions, and economic activities.

Metaverses like Decentraland, Cryptovoxels, and Roblox have gained significant attention and popularity. These metaverses provide users with the ability to own, trade, and develop virtual properties within their digital realms. Users can create virtual businesses, host virtual events, engage in virtual commerce, and even monetize their digital creations. Metaverses have their own economies and virtual property markets, allowing users to buy, sell, and rent virtual real estate for profit or personal enjoyment.

The potential of metaverses goes beyond entertainment and gaming. They have attracted the attention of industries such as real estate, fashion, art, and advertising. Real estate companies are exploring the development of virtual properties that mimic real-world locations, providing virtual tours and experiences. Fashion brands are designing virtual clothing and accessories for users to personalize their avatars. Artists are showcasing and selling digital art within metaverses, opening up new avenues for creativity and monetization.

Metaverses also hold promise for virtual events and collaborations. Companies can host virtual conferences, trade shows, and product launches within these immersive environments, reaching a global audience without the limitations of physical venues. Collaborations between brands and metaverses offer unique opportunities for innovative marketing campaigns and experiential activations.

It is important to note that the concept of metaverses is still evolving, and there are ongoing discussions and explorations regarding their standards, interoperability, and governance. However, the growing interest and investments in metaverses indicate their potential to shape the future of digital real estate and redefine how we interact, work, and conduct business in virtual spaces.

In conclusion, virtual real estate and metaverses have opened up a new frontier in the realm of digital real estate. The ability to own, create, and trade virtual properties within virtual worlds and metaverses presents exciting opportunities for individuals and businesses. From virtual commerce to immersive experiences, virtual real estate and metaverses offer a unique blend of creativity, social interaction, and economic potential.

Chapter 3: Researching and Evaluating Digital Properties

3.1 Market Analysis and Trends

In the realm of digital properties, conducting a comprehensive market analysis is essential for understanding the market landscape and identifying current trends. Market analysis provides valuable insights that can inform your investment decisions and help you capitalize on emerging opportunities. Let's explore the key aspects of market analysis and trends.

a. Market Size and Growth: Begin by assessing the size of the digital real estate market and its growth potential. Consider factors such as the number of internet users, the adoption of digital technologies, and the overall market value. Market research reports, industry publications, and reputable data sources can provide valuable information to understand the market's current state and projected growth.

b. Competitive Analysis: Analyzing the competitive landscape is crucial to identify key players and competitors in the market. Examine their digital properties, business models, marketing strategies, and market share. By understanding the strengths and weaknesses of your competitors, you can identify gaps and opportunities for differentiation.

c. Industry Trends: Stay up-to-date with the latest industry trends in digital properties. Technology is constantly evolving, and new trends emerge regularly. Stay informed about advancements in areas such as virtual reality, augmented reality, artificial intelligence, blockchain, and other relevant technologies. Identify how these trends can impact the value, functionality, and demand for different types of digital properties.

d. User Behavior and Demographics: Analyzing user behavior and demographics is vital for understanding your target audience. Identify the preferences, needs, and behaviors of your potential users or customers. Consider factors like age, gender, interests, online habits, and the devices they use. This information will help you tailor your digital properties to meet the expectations and demands of your target audience.

e. Emerging Opportunities: As you conduct market analysis, keep an eye out for emerging opportunities. Look for untapped niches, underserved markets, or innovative approaches that can set your digital properties apart. Emerging technologies, shifting consumer behaviors, or changing market dynamics can present new opportunities for growth and differentiation.

Market analysis provides a foundation for strategic decision-making in the digital real estate market. By understanding the market size, growth potential, competitive landscape, industry trends, user behavior, and emerging opportunities, you can position your digital properties for success and stay ahead of the curve.

conducting a thorough market analysis and staying abreast of industry trends are critical steps when researching and evaluating digital properties. By understanding the market landscape, identifying trends, and staying informed about emerging opportunities, you can make informed investment decisions and develop digital properties that resonate with your target audience.

3.2 Assessing the Potential Value of Online Properties

When evaluating online properties, it is crucial to assess their potential value accurately. Understanding the value of digital properties will help you make informed decisions about investments, acquisitions, or strategic planning. Let's explore the key factors to consider when assessing the potential value of online properties.

a. Traffic and User Engagement: Evaluate the level of traffic and user engagement the online property receives. Analyze website analytics, social media metrics, and user behavior data to understand the property's reach, popularity, and user interaction. Consider metrics such as page views, unique visitors, time spent on site, click-through rates, social media followers, and engagement rates. Higher traffic and engagement indicate a more valuable online property.

b. Monetization Strategies: Assess the property's current and potential monetization strategies. Evaluate the revenue streams it utilizes or has the potential to incorporate. This may include advertising, sponsorships, subscriptions, e-commerce sales, affiliate marketing, or premium content offerings. Understand the property's revenue model and its potential for generating consistent and sustainable income.

c. Branding and Reputation: Evaluate the strength of the property's brand and reputation. A strong brand, positive reputation, and loyal user base contribute significantly to the value of an online property. Assess factors such as brand recognition, customer satisfaction, online reviews, and overall perception in the market. A trusted and respected brand enhances the potential value and growth prospects of the property.

d. Intellectual Property and Unique Assets: Identify any intellectual property or unique assets associated with the online property. This could include proprietary technology, patents, trademarks, copyrights, exclusive content, or a valuable user database. Such assets can enhance the property's value and differentiate it from competitors.

e. Growth Potential: Assess the growth potential of the online property. Consider factors such as market demand, competitive landscape, industry trends, and the property's ability to scale and adapt. Analyze future growth opportunities, expansion possibilities, and the property's potential to capitalize on emerging trends or user needs.

f. Financial Performance: Conduct a financial assessment of the online property. Evaluate its revenue, expenses, profitability, and financial projections. Analyze the historical financial performance and assess its potential for sustainable growth. Consider factors such as revenue growth rate, profit margins, cost structure, and cash flow.

g. Market Comparisons: Compare the online property to similar properties in the market. Analyze how it measures up against competitors in terms of traffic, user engagement, monetization strategies, branding, and other relevant factors. This comparison will provide insights into the property's relative value and competitive position.

By considering these factors, you can evaluate the potential value of online properties more accurately. Keep in mind that value assessment is subjective and can vary based on industry dynamics, market conditions, and individual goals. Conducting thorough research and analysis will help you make informed decisions and maximize the potential of your online properties.

assessing the potential value of online properties requires a comprehensive evaluation of factors such as traffic, user engagement, monetization strategies, branding, intellectual property, growth potential, financial performance, and market comparisons. By understanding these aspects, you can make informed decisions about investments, acquisitions, or strategic actions related to online properties.

Here's a step-by-step guide to assessing the potential value of online properties:

Step 1: Gather Data and Metrics

Collect relevant data and metrics about the online property you are evaluating. This includes website analytics, social media metrics, user behavior data, revenue figures, and any other relevant performance indicators. Ensure you have a comprehensive understanding of the property's current state.

Step 2: Evaluate Traffic and User Engagement

Analyze the level of traffic the online property receives. Examine metrics such as page views, unique visitors, and time spent on site. Assess user engagement metrics like click-through rates, social media followers, and engagement rates. Higher traffic and engagement indicate a more valuable online property.

Step 3: Assess Monetization Strategies

Evaluate the property's current and potential monetization strategies. Understand the revenue streams it currently utilizes, such as advertising, subscriptions, e-commerce sales, or affiliate marketing. Assess the property's revenue model and its potential for generating consistent and sustainable income.

Step 4: Consider Branding and Reputation

Evaluate the strength of the property's brand and reputation. Assess factors such as brand recognition, customer satisfaction, online reviews, and overall perception in the market. A strong brand and positive reputation contribute significantly to the value of an online property.

Step 5: Identify Intellectual Property and Unique Assets

Identify any intellectual property or unique assets associated with the online property. This could include proprietary technology, patents, trademarks, copyrights, exclusive content, or a valuable user database.

Such assets can enhance the property's value and differentiate it from competitors.

Step 6: Assess Growth Potential

Evaluate the growth potential of the online property. Consider factors such as market demand, competitive landscape, industry trends, and the property's ability to scale and adapt. Analyze future growth opportunities, expansion possibilities, and the property's potential to capitalize on emerging trends or user needs.

Step 7: Conduct a Financial Assessment

Evaluate the financial performance of the online property. Assess its revenue, expenses, profitability, and financial projections. Analyze the historical financial performance and assess its potential for sustainable growth. Consider factors such as revenue growth rate, profit margins, cost structure, and cash flow.

Step 8: Perform Market Comparisons

Compare the online property to similar properties in the market. Analyze how it measures up against competitors in terms of traffic, user engagement, monetization strategies, branding, and other relevant factors. This comparison will provide insights into the property's relative value and competitive position.

Step 9: Synthesize Findings and Make an Evaluation

Take all the data, metrics, and insights gathered from the previous steps and synthesize them to form an evaluation of the potential value of the online property. Consider all the factors, weigh their importance, and make an informed assessment of the property's value.

Remember that value assessment is subjective and can vary based on industry dynamics, market conditions, and individual goals. The steps outlined here provide a structured approach to assessing the potential value of online properties, but adapt them as needed based on your specific circumstances and requirements.

By following these steps, you can conduct a comprehensive evaluation of the potential value of online properties, helping you make informed decisions about investments, acquisitions, or strategic actions related to digital assets.

3.3 Due Diligence and Risk Assessment

When considering digital properties for investment or acquisition, conducting due diligence and risk assessment is crucial to mitigate potential risks and make informed decisions. Let's explore the step-by-step process of due diligence and risk assessment for digital properties.

Step 1: Legal and Regulatory Compliance

Ensure the digital property complies with applicable laws, regulations, and industry standards. Review contracts, licenses, and agreements associated with the property to identify any potential legal liabilities or intellectual property infringement risks. Consult legal professionals specialized in digital property transactions if necessary.

Step 2: Technical Assessment

Evaluate the technical aspects of the digital property. Assess its infrastructure, security measures, scalability, and compatibility with different platforms and devices. Identify any potential technical vulnerabilities or limitations that may impact the property's performance or security. Engage technical experts or consultants if needed.

Step 3: Financial Assessment

Conduct a thorough financial analysis of the digital property. Review financial statements, revenue figures, expense breakdowns, and cash flow statements. Analyze the property's profitability, growth trajectory, and financial projections. Identify any financial risks or concerns that may impact the property's value or future performance.

Step 4: User Data and Privacy

Assess how the digital property handles user data and privacy. Ensure it adheres to data protection regulations and has appropriate security measures in place to protect user information. Evaluate the property's privacy policy, data storage practices, and any history of data breaches or security incidents.

Step 5: Market and Competitive Analysis

Perform a comprehensive market analysis, as discussed in Chapter 3.1, to assess market trends, competitive landscape, and potential risks related to market volatility or shifts in user behavior. Identify competitors and evaluate their strategies, market share, and potential impact on the digital property's success.

Step 6: Reputation and Online Presence

Research the digital property's online reputation and presence. Analyze user reviews, customer feedback, and social media sentiment. Look for any negative press, controversies, or customer complaints that may impact the property's reputation and user trust. Assess the property's brand image and how it aligns with your investment goals.

Step 7: Operational and Strategic Risks

Identify and evaluate operational and strategic risks associated with the digital property. Consider factors such as dependency on key personnel, reliance on specific technologies or platforms, potential disruption from emerging competitors or market shifts, and scalability challenges. Assess how these risks may impact the property's long-term viability.

Step 8: Exit Strategy and Future Plans

Consider the potential for exit strategies or future plans related to the digital property. Assess the property's transferability, market demand for similar properties, and potential for growth or diversification. Evaluate how well the property aligns with your investment goals and future plans for the digital real estate market.

Step 9: Synthesize Findings and Make an Informed Decision

Synthesize all the information and insights gathered during the due diligence and risk assessment process. Consider the potential risks, legal compliance, financial health, market dynamics, reputation, and operational aspects of the digital property. Based on this analysis, make an informed decision about proceeding with the investment or acquisition, adjusting terms, or seeking further clarification or negotiations.

By following these steps, you can perform due diligence and risk assessment for digital properties, ensuring a comprehensive evaluation of potential risks and opportunities. Remember to adapt the process to your specific needs and seek professional advice or guidance when necessary. Making informed decisions based on thorough due diligence will help you mitigate risks and maximize the potential of your investments in the dynamic world of digital properties.

Chapter 4: Monetization Strategies for Digital Properties

4.1 Advertising and Affiliate Marketing

Advertising and affiliate marketing are popular monetization strategies for digital properties. Let's explore how these strategies can generate revenue.

Advertising: By displaying advertisements on your digital property, you can earn revenue based on various models, such as cost per click (CPC), cost per mille (CPM), or cost per action (CPA). Advertising networks like Google AdSense or Media.net provide a platform to connect advertisers with publishers. You can choose between display ads, native ads, video ads, or sponsored content depending on your digital property's format and user experience.

Affiliate Marketing: With affiliate marketing, you can promote products or services through your digital property and earn a commission for every successful referral or sale. Joining affiliate programs from platforms like Amazon Associates, ShareASale, or Commission Junction allows you to access a wide range of products and services to promote. Incorporate affiliate links within your content or utilize dedicated affiliate marketing plugins to track and monetize your referrals.

4.2 E-commerce and Dropshipping

E-commerce and dropshipping enable you to sell products directly through your digital property. Consider the following approaches:

E-commerce: Create an online store within your digital property to sell physical or digital products. Platforms like Shopify, WooCommerce, or Magento provide robust e-commerce solutions that allow you to manage inventory, process payments, and fulfill orders. You have full control over product selection, pricing, and customer experience.

Dropshipping: Alternatively, you can leverage dropshipping to sell products without managing inventory or shipping. With dropshipping, you partner with suppliers who handle product storage and fulfillment. When a customer makes a purchase through your digital property, the supplier ships the product directly to the customer. Platforms like Oberlo, Spocket, or AliExpress can facilitate dropshipping integration within your digital property.

4.3 Content Creation and Licensing

Creating and licensing digital content can be a lucrative monetization strategy. Consider the following approaches:

Digital Products: Develop and sell digital products like e-books, online courses, software, templates, or graphics. Leverage your expertise and unique insights to provide valuable content that meets the needs of your target audience. Platforms like Teachable or Gumroad can assist in creating and selling digital products.

Premium Content and Memberships: Offer premium content or exclusive memberships that provide additional value to your audience. This can include access to in-depth articles, videos, podcasts, or community forums. Implement a subscription-based model or create tiered membership levels to monetize this content effectively.

Licensing and Syndication: If you produce high-quality content, you can license it to other platforms, publications, or media outlets. Syndication allows your content to reach a broader audience, and you can earn revenue through licensing fees or revenue sharing agreements.

4.4 Virtual Real Estate Rentals and Leasing

For virtual real estate within metaverses or virtual worlds, rentals and leasing can be a monetization strategy. Consider the following approaches:

Virtual Property Rentals: If you own virtual properties within metaverses, you can rent them out to other users for various purposes. This can include hosting virtual events, showcasing virtual art or exhibitions, or providing virtual office spaces. Establish rental agreements, pricing models, and offer value-added services to maximize revenue.

Advertising and Sponsorships: Within virtual properties, you can integrate advertising placements or offer sponsorships to brands or businesses. This can include virtual billboards, branded spaces, or product placements. Collaborate with advertisers to create engaging and immersive advertising experiences within the virtual environment.

Virtual Asset Sales and Trading: Buy, develop, and sell virtual properties within metaverses. As the popularity and value of metaverses grow, there is a potential market for trading virtual assets. Acquire desirable virtual properties and resell them at a higher price, similar to real estate investment.

In conclusion, various monetization strategies can help generate revenue from digital properties. Advertising and affiliate marketing allow you to earn through partnerships with advertisers. E-commerce and dropshipping enable direct product sales. Content creation and licensing provide opportunities to sell digital products or license content. Virtual real estate rentals and leasing capitalize on the emerging market of virtual worlds. Depending on your digital property's nature and target audience, you can choose one or a combination of these strategies to effectively monetize your assets.

Chapter 5: Strategies for Acquiring Digital Properties

5.1 Auctions, Marketplaces, and Brokers

When it comes to acquiring digital properties, there are various avenues to explore, including auctions, marketplaces, and working with brokers. Let's delve into each strategy and understand how they can help you in acquiring digital properties.

Auctions:

Online auctions specifically tailored for buying and selling digital properties can be an effective way to acquire assets. Platforms like Flippa, Empire Flippers, Sedo, or Namecheap Auctions host auctions where you can bid on websites, domain names, apps, or other digital assets. Participating in auctions allows you to access a wide range of properties and engage in competitive bidding. It's important to thoroughly research and evaluate properties before participating in an auction to ensure you're making informed bids.

Marketplaces:

Online marketplaces dedicated to digital properties provide a centralized platform where buyers and sellers can connect. Platforms like DigitalPoint, BuySellAds, WebsiteBroker, or even specialized forums and communities offer listings of websites, domain names, and other digital assets for sale. These marketplaces provide a convenient way to browse, compare, and communicate with sellers. They often provide tools and resources to facilitate the buying process, such as escrow services for secure transactions. Regularly monitor these marketplaces to stay updated on available properties and engage with sellers.

Brokers:

Working with professional brokers who specialize in digital property transactions can offer several advantages. These brokers have expertise in evaluating, valuing, and negotiating deals on behalf of buyers. They can assist in identifying suitable properties, conducting due diligence, and handling the transaction process. They have established relationships with sellers and can provide access to off-market or exclusive opportunities. Research and select reputable brokers with a track record in the digital property market. Ensure they have a clear understanding of your investment goals and can effectively represent your interests.

When utilizing auctions, marketplaces, or brokers, keep the following considerations in mind:

- Thoroughly research the platform or broker's reputation and track record. Look for reviews, testimonials, or case studies from previous clients to gauge their credibility and success rate.
- Understand the fees and commissions associated with using these services. Auctions and marketplaces may charge listing fees or take a percentage of the final sale price, while brokers may have their own fee structure.
- Clearly define your investment criteria and goals. This will help

you filter and evaluate properties more effectively, allowing you to focus on opportunities that align with your objectives.

- Conduct due diligence on any property you're interested in. Evaluate its performance, traffic, revenue, and potential risks to ensure it meets your investment requirements.
- Be prepared for competition, especially in auctions or highly sought-after marketplaces. Set a budget and bidding strategy to avoid overpaying or getting caught up in a bidding war.

Utilizing auctions, marketplaces, or brokers can provide access to a wide range of digital properties and facilitate the acquisition process. However, it's important to approach each opportunity with a critical eye, conduct thorough due diligence, and negotiate with care to ensure you make informed decisions and acquire properties that align with your investment objectives.

5.2 Identifying Profitable Investment Opportunities

Identifying profitable investment opportunities is crucial when acquiring digital properties. By conducting thorough research and analysis, you can increase your chances of acquiring assets that align with your investment goals and have the potential for growth and profitability. Here are some strategies to help you identify profitable investment opportunities:

Market Research:
Conduct comprehensive market research to identify emerging trends, niche markets, or high-growth sectors within the digital property industry. Stay updated on industry news, technological advancements,

and shifts in user behavior. This knowledge will help you spot investment opportunities before they become saturated or mainstream. Look for data, reports, and insights from reputable sources, industry publications, or specialized market research firms.

Scouting Platforms:

Regularly monitor online platforms, forums, and communities where digital properties are discussed. Platforms like Reddit, niche-specific forums, or social media groups can provide valuable insights and discussions about potential investment opportunities. Engage in conversations, ask questions, and network with industry professionals to discover hidden gems or upcoming opportunities. These platforms can also help you identify distressed or undervalued assets that may present investment potential.

Networking and Relationships:

Building relationships within the digital property industry can provide access to exclusive investment opportunities. Attend industry conferences, join online communities, and connect with other investors, brokers, or professionals. Networking allows you to stay informed about potential deals, receive referrals, and gain insights from experienced individuals in the field. Collaborating with others may also open up opportunities for joint ventures or partnerships.

Analyzing Potential:

Evaluate potential investment opportunities based on various criteria. Consider factors such as traffic, revenue potential, growth prospects, market trends, and monetization strategies. Analyze historical performance data, future projections, and compare properties within the same market segment. Conduct thorough due diligence to assess the risks and potential rewards of each opportunity. Define your investment criteria and prioritize properties that align with your goals, risk tolerance, and available resources.

Stay Agile and Flexible:

The digital property market is dynamic, and opportunities can arise unexpectedly. Stay agile and flexible in your approach. Be open to exploring different types of digital properties, including websites, domain names, apps, or virtual real estate. Adapt your strategies as market conditions and trends evolve. Be prepared to pivot and adjust your investment focus based on new opportunities or emerging sectors.

Seek Professional Advice:

Consider seeking professional advice from experts in the digital property industry. Engage consultants, brokers, or investment advisors who specialize in digital properties. They can provide valuable insights, conduct market analysis, and help identify profitable investment opportunities. Their expertise and experience can guide you in making informed decisions and increasing your chances of successful acquisitions.

By utilizing these strategies, conducting thorough research, and staying informed about market trends, you can identify profitable investment opportunities in the digital property market. Remember that each opportunity should be evaluated based on your investment criteria, risk appetite, and long-term goals. Careful analysis and due diligence will help you make informed decisions and maximize the potential for profitability.

5.3 Negotiating and Closing Deals

Negotiating and closing deals effectively is crucial when acquiring digital properties. Here are some strategies to help you navigate the negotiation process and successfully close deals:

Understand the Seller's Motivations: Take the time to understand the seller's motivations for selling the digital property. Are they looking for a quick sale, facing financial challenges, or exploring new opportunities? Understanding their motivations can help you tailor your negotiation strategy and identify areas of potential flexibility.

Determine Your Walk-Away Point: Define your walk-away point, which is the maximum price or terms you are willing to accept for the acquisition. Establishing this beforehand helps you stay objective during negotiations and avoid making emotionally-driven decisions. Stick to your walk-away point unless there are compelling reasons to reconsider.

Research and Preparation: Conduct thorough research on the digital property, including its traffic, revenue, market comparables, and potential risks. This information strengthens your negotiation position and allows you to make well-informed offers. Prepare a solid argument backed by data and insights to support your proposed terms.

Build Rapport and Establish Trust: Establishing a positive rapport with the seller is important for effective negotiation. Engage in open and honest communication, actively listen to the seller's perspective, and be respectful throughout the process. Building trust creates a conducive environment for reaching mutually beneficial agreements.

Focus on Value, Not Just Price: While price is a significant aspect of negotiations, it's essential to consider the overall value of the digital property. Highlight the value you bring as a buyer, such as your expertise, resources, or plans for growth. Demonstrate how your acquisition can benefit the seller and contribute to the property's long-term success.

Explore Creative Solutions: Be open to creative solutions that benefit both parties. This could include structuring the deal with flexible payment terms, earn-outs based on performance, or including non-monetary incentives. Collaborative problem-solving can lead to win-win outcomes and facilitate smoother negotiations.

Conduct Due Diligence: Before finalizing the deal, conduct thorough due diligence to verify the property's claims, data, and legal compliance. Review financial records, traffic analytics, user engagement metrics, and any other relevant documentation. Engage professionals if needed, such as legal experts or technical consultants, to ensure a comprehensive evaluation.

Formalize the Agreement: Once negotiations are complete, formalize the agreement in a purchase agreement or contract. Clearly outline the terms and conditions, including the purchase price, payment structure, transfer of assets, non-compete clauses, and any additional provisions. Consult legal professionals to ensure all legal requirements are met and protect your interests.

Close the Deal: Coordinate with the seller to complete the closing process. Ensure a smooth transfer of assets, domains, or any associated accounts. Execute the payment as agreed upon in the purchase agreement. Follow any necessary legal or regulatory requirements, such as transferring domain registrations or updating ownership details.

Maintain Professionalism: Throughout the negotiation and closing process, maintain professionalism and integrity. Be responsive, prompt, and respectful in your communication. Even if negotiations become challenging, focus on finding common ground and reaching a mutually beneficial agreement.

By applying these strategies, you can navigate negotiations effectively and increase your chances of successfully closing deals for acquiring digital properties. Remember to prioritize transparency, professionalism, and win-win outcomes to build positive relationships and establish a strong foundation for future opportunities.

Chapter 6: Managing and Optimizing Digital Properties

6.1 Website Development and Optimization

Managing and optimizing your website is essential for maximizing its performance and user experience. Here are some key strategies to consider:

a. Regular Updates: Keep your website content fresh and up-to-date. Regularly add new content, update information, and remove outdated or irrelevant elements. This shows visitors that your website is active and maintained.

b. User Experience (UX) Optimization: Focus on providing a seamless and intuitive user experience. Optimize website navigation, ensure fast loading times, and make the layout visually appealing.

Conduct user testing and gather feedback to identify areas for improvement.

c. Search Engine Optimization (SEO): Implement SEO strategies to improve your website's visibility in search engine results. Conduct keyword research, optimize meta tags, headers, and content, and build high-quality backlinks. Regularly monitor SEO performance and adjust strategies accordingly.

d. Mobile Optimization: With the increasing use of mobile devices, optimize your website for mobile responsiveness. Ensure it displays properly on various screen sizes and loads quickly on mobile devices. Mobile optimization enhances user experience and improves search engine rankings.

e. Conversion Rate Optimization (CRO): Continuously analyze and optimize your website to improve conversion rates. Use A/B testing, optimize call-to-action buttons, and streamline the checkout process. Monitor user behavior through analytics and make data-driven decisions to optimize conversions.

6.2 Social Media Management and Engagement

Effective social media management can enhance your digital property's visibility, engagement, and brand presence. Consider the following strategies:

a. Consistent Branding: Maintain consistent branding across your social media channels. Use consistent profile images, cover photos, and brand messaging. Ensure your social media presence reflects your overall brand identity.

b. Content Strategy: Develop a content strategy that aligns with your target audience and business goals. Create and share relevant, valuable content that resonates with your followers. Use a mix of text, images, videos, and interactive elements to keep your audience engaged.

c. Active Engagement: Actively engage with your audience by responding to comments, messages, and mentions. Encourage dialogue, ask questions, and participate in relevant conversations. Building relationships with your followers fosters loyalty and encourages them to share your content.

d. Influencer Partnerships: Collaborate with influencers or industry experts to expand your reach and credibility. Identify influencers relevant to your niche and engage in mutually beneficial partnerships, such as sponsored content or guest collaborations. Influencers can help amplify your message and attract new followers.

e. Performance Tracking: Monitor and analyze social media metrics to measure the effectiveness of your efforts. Track metrics such as follower growth, engagement rates, reach, and conversions. Use this data to refine your social media strategies and identify areas for improvement.

6.3 Virtual Real Estate Maintenance and Enhancement

Managing and enhancing virtual real estate within metaverses or virtual worlds requires ongoing attention. Consider the following strategies:

a. Regular Updates and Maintenance: Regularly maintain and update your virtual property to ensure it remains relevant and appealing to users. Implement new features, improve aesthetics, and fix any technical issues promptly. Respond to user feedback and suggestions for continuous improvement.

b. Community Engagement: Foster a sense of community within your virtual property. Encourage user participation, organize events, and create interactive experiences. Engage with users through chat, forums, or virtual social spaces to build a vibrant community.

c. Monetization Opportunities: Explore additional monetization opportunities within your virtual property. This could include virtual goods or services, sponsorship opportunities, or in-world advertising. Continuously evaluate the market and adapt your monetization strategies to maximize revenue.

d. Collaboration and Partnerships: Seek collaboration opportunities with other virtual property owners, businesses, or organizations within the metaverse. Collaborative events or cross-promotions can attract a larger audience and enhance the overall experience for users.

e. Integration with Emerging Technologies: Stay updated with emerging technologies and trends within the virtual space. Explore opportunities to integrate technologies like virtual reality, augmented reality, or blockchain to enhance the functionality and user experience of your virtual property.

By implementing these strategies, you can effectively manage and optimize your digital properties, whether it's a website, social media presence, or virtual real estate. Continuously monitoring performance, engaging with your audience, and adapting to emerging trends will help you stay competitive and maximize the potential of your digital assets.

Chapter 7: Growing Your Digital Real Estate Portfolio

7.1 Diversification and Risk Management

Diversification and risk management are essential strategies for growing and safeguarding your digital real estate portfolio. Here's a closer look at how you can effectively implement these strategies:

Diversify Asset Types: Invest in a variety of digital assets to spread your risk and increase potential returns. Consider acquiring websites, domain names, apps, virtual real estate, or other emerging digital properties. Diversifying your portfolio across different asset types allows you to mitigate the impact of market fluctuations in any particular sector.

Geographic Diversification: Expand your portfolio across different geographic regions. By investing in digital properties in diverse markets, you can reduce the risk associated with regional economic downturns, regulatory changes, or market-specific risks. Assess the potential of different markets and consider properties that can provide exposure to multiple regions.

Niche Diversification: Explore opportunities in different niches or industries. By diversifying across niches, you reduce the risk of being heavily reliant on a single market segment. Analyze trends, market demand, and growth potential in various niches to identify investment opportunities that align with your risk tolerance and growth objectives.

Risk Assessment and Due Diligence: Conduct thorough risk assessments and due diligence before acquiring any digital property. Evaluate factors such as market stability, competition, revenue streams, growth potential, and legal considerations. Identify potential risks and develop mitigation strategies to protect your investments. Engage professionals if needed, such as legal experts or industry consultants, to conduct in-depth assessments.

Risk Hedging: Consider hedging strategies to manage risks within your digital real estate portfolio. This can involve acquiring assets that have negative correlation or perform differently in various market conditions. For example, if you own properties in competitive niches, you could acquire assets in less competitive or emerging markets to balance your risk exposure.

Monitor and Adjust: Continuously monitor the performance of your digital properties and regularly assess their risk profiles. Stay updated on market trends, technological advancements, and regulatory changes that may impact your investments. Make informed decisions about portfolio rebalancing or divestment based on changing market conditions or the performance of individual assets.

Insurance and Legal Protection: Explore insurance options specific to digital assets and consult legal professionals to protect your portfolio. Cybersecurity insurance can help mitigate the financial risks associated with data breaches or cyberattacks. Additionally, legal experts can assist in structuring contracts, addressing intellectual property issues, and ensuring compliance with applicable laws and regulations.

Portfolio Size and Allocation: Consider the size and allocation of your portfolio to manage risk effectively. Avoid over-concentration in a few high-value assets, as this can increase vulnerability to market fluctuations or individual asset risks. Strive for a balanced portfolio that provides diversification and aligns with your risk tolerance and investment objectives.

Remember that diversification does not guarantee a profit or protect against losses, but it is a risk management strategy that can help reduce the impact of individual asset performance. Regularly assess the risk-reward profile of your portfolio and make adjustments as needed to maintain a healthy and balanced investment mix.

By implementing diversification and risk management strategies, you can mitigate risks and increase the potential for growth and stability in your digital real estate portfolio. Careful evaluation, ongoing monitoring, and a proactive approach to risk management will help you build a resilient and successful portfolio in the digital property market.

7.2 Scaling and Leveraging Your Investments

Scaling and leveraging your investments are strategies that can help you maximize returns and expand your digital real estate portfolio. Here are some key strategies to consider:

Scaling Existing Properties:

Focus on scaling and optimizing the performance of your existing digital properties. Continuously analyze and improve revenue streams, user experience, and marketing strategies to increase traffic, engagement, and profitability. Identify opportunities for growth within your current portfolio and implement strategies to capitalize on them.

Strategic Acquisitions:

Look for strategic acquisition opportunities that align with your investment goals and portfolio strategy. Seek out undervalued or underperforming digital properties that have the potential for improvement. Conduct thorough due diligence to identify properties that can complement and enhance your existing portfolio.

Leveraging Financing Options:

Explore financing options to leverage your investments. Consider obtaining loans, lines of credit, or securing partnerships to fund acquisitions. Assess the financial implications, interest rates, and repayment terms to ensure that leveraging aligns with your long-term goals and risk tolerance. Carefully manage your leverage to avoid excessive debt and maintain financial stability.

Joint Ventures and Partnerships:

Forming joint ventures or partnerships with other investors or industry experts can provide opportunities for growth and expansion. Pooling resources, knowledge, and expertise can help you undertake larger acquisitions, access new markets, and share risks. Collaborative efforts can accelerate the growth of your digital real estate portfolio and open doors to new opportunities.

Scalable Business Models:

Invest in digital properties with scalable business models. Look for properties that have the potential for exponential growth and can scale without significantly increasing costs. Seek out opportunities with recurring revenue streams, automation potential, or the ability to expand into related markets. Scalable business models allow for long-term growth and increased value within your portfolio.

Strategic Management:

Implement effective management strategies to optimize the performance of your portfolio. Continuously monitor and evaluate the performance of each digital property. Identify areas for improvement, such as optimizing monetization strategies, enhancing user experience, or expanding target markets. Regularly review and adjust your portfolio composition to align with changing market dynamics and emerging opportunities.

Long-Term Vision and Sustainability:

Maintain a long-term vision for your portfolio and focus on sustainable growth. Consider both short-term gains and long-term value creation when making investment decisions. Strive for a balance between immediate returns and investments with long-term growth potential. Continuously evaluate market trends, technological advancements, and user preferences to adapt and evolve your portfolio strategy.

Professional Advisory:

Seek professional advice from experts in the digital real estate industry. Engage consultants, investment advisors, or legal professionals who specialize in digital properties. They can provide valuable insights, assess investment opportunities, and guide you in developing effective scaling and leveraging strategies. Their expertise can help you navigate complex transactions, assess risks, and optimize your portfolio for growth.

By implementing these strategies, you can effectively scale and leverage your investments to grow your digital real estate portfolio. Remember to assess opportunities carefully, manage risks, and maintain a long-term perspective. Continuously evaluate and adjust your strategies to align with market conditions and emerging trends. With a strategic approach, you can expand your portfolio and increase its profitability over time.

7.3 Strategies for Long-Term Growth and Sustainability

To ensure long-term growth and sustainability of your digital real estate portfolio, it's important to implement strategies that focus on stability, value creation, and adaptability. Here are some key strategies to consider:

Step: Set Clear Long-Term Objectives:

Define your long-term objectives for your portfolio. Identify specific goals, such as the desired portfolio size, target returns, or a timeline for achieving certain milestones. Having clear objectives will guide your decision-making and help you stay focused on sustainable growth.

Step: Continuously Monitor Market Trends:

Stay updated on market trends, emerging technologies, and industry developments. Regularly monitor market dynamics, shifts in user behavior, and changes in demand. This knowledge will enable you to adapt your portfolio strategy to seize new opportunities and stay ahead of the competition.

Step: Foster Innovation and Adaptability:

Encourage innovation and adaptability within your portfolio. Embrace new technologies, trends, and business models that have the potential to disrupt or enhance the digital real estate industry. Continuously explore ways to leverage emerging technologies and stay at the forefront of innovation.

Step: Foster User Engagement and Satisfaction:

Focus on providing exceptional user experiences across your digital properties. Prioritize user satisfaction and engagement by delivering valuable content, intuitive navigation, and responsive customer support. Cultivate a strong brand reputation that fosters loyalty and encourages repeat visits or transactions.

Step: Build Sustainable Monetization Strategies:

Develop sustainable monetization strategies for your digital properties. Focus on revenue streams that provide long-term stability and growth. Explore diverse monetization methods such as advertising, affiliate marketing, e-commerce, subscriptions, or licensing. Continuously evaluate and optimize your monetization strategies based on market trends and user preferences.

Step: Embrace Data-Driven Decision Making:

Leverage data and analytics to drive informed decision-making. Regularly analyze key metrics and performance indicators to evaluate the success of your digital properties. Utilize tools and technologies to track user behavior, traffic sources, conversion rates, and other relevant data points. Make data-driven decisions to optimize your portfolio performance.

Step: Seek Strategic Partnerships:

Explore strategic partnerships and collaborations within the digital real estate industry. Partnering with other industry players can open doors to new markets, technologies, or investment opportunities. Identify synergies and shared goals with potential partners and develop mutually beneficial relationships that contribute to your long-term growth.

Step: Plan for Exit Strategies:

Develop exit strategies for your digital properties. Consider long-term goals, such as selling certain properties at a profitable valuation, transitioning to passive income streams, or exiting specific markets. Having exit strategies in place allows you to capitalize on favorable market conditions or adapt to changing circumstances.

Step: Stay Compliant and Ethical:

Maintain compliance with applicable laws, regulations, and ethical standards. Stay informed about legal requirements related to data privacy, intellectual property rights, advertising practices, and other relevant aspects of the digital real estate industry. Conduct business with integrity and prioritize the trust of your users and stakeholders.

Step: Regularly Review and Rebalance:

Regularly review your portfolio composition and performance. Assess the alignment of your properties with your long-term objectives and make necessary adjustments. Rebalance your portfolio by divesting underperforming assets or acquiring new properties that better fit your investment strategy and growth objectives.

By implementing these strategies for long-term growth and sustainability, you can build a resilient and successful digital real estate portfolio. Remember to regularly evaluate market trends, prioritize user satisfaction, innovate, and adapt to stay ahead in the ever-evolving digital landscape. Continuously monitor the performance of your properties and make data-driven decisions to optimize your portfolio for long-term success.

Chapter 8: Navigating Legal and Ethical Considerations

8.1 Intellectual Property and Copyrights

Intellectual property (IP) and copyrights are critical considerations when dealing with digital properties. Here are key aspects to navigate:

a. Copyright Ownership: Understand copyright laws and ensure you have the proper ownership or licensing rights for any content or creative works associated with your digital properties. Respect the copyrights of others and obtain necessary permissions or licenses when using copyrighted material.

b. Trademarks and Branding: Protect your own trademarks and branding elements associated with your digital properties. Conduct thorough trademark searches before adopting a new brand or domain name to avoid infringing on existing trademarks. Safeguard your brand identity and take action against any instances of infringement.

c. Fair Use and Copyright Exceptions: Familiarize yourself with fair use and other copyright exceptions that allow for the limited use of copyrighted material without permission. However, be cautious to avoid overstepping these exceptions and seek legal advice if you are uncertain about the boundaries.

d. DMCA Compliance: Understand the Digital Millennium Copyright Act (DMCA) requirements, especially if you provide platforms for user-generated content. Implement proper procedures for responding to copyright infringement claims and take necessary actions to remove infringing material from your platforms.

e. License Agreements: When acquiring digital properties, review and assess any existing license agreements for content, software, or other intellectual property assets. Ensure that the licenses are valid, properly transferred, and compliant with relevant copyright laws.

8.2 Privacy and Data Protection

Privacy and data protection are essential considerations to protect user information and comply with regulations. Here are important factors to navigate:

a. Data Collection and Consent: Clearly disclose and obtain user consent for the collection, use, and storage of personal data associated with your digital properties. Comply with applicable data protection laws, such as the General Data Protection Regulation (GDPR) or the California Consumer Privacy Act (CCPA).

b. Data Security: Implement robust security measures to safeguard user data from unauthorized access, breaches, or misuse. Follow best practices in encryption, secure storage, access controls, and regular security audits to maintain data integrity and user trust.

c. Privacy Policies: Create and maintain comprehensive privacy policies that clearly communicate how user data is collected, used, and shared. Ensure that your policies are accessible, easy to understand, and aligned with relevant regulations.

d. Cookie Compliance: Comply with cookie laws and provide transparent information about the use of cookies or similar tracking technologies. Offer mechanisms for users to manage cookie preferences and obtain their consent when required.

e. International Data Transfers: If your digital properties involve international data transfers, ensure compliance with applicable regulations, such as the EU-US Privacy Shield framework or Standard Contractual Clauses (SCCs), to provide adequate protection for personal data.

8.3 Compliance and Regulations

Adhering to applicable laws and regulations is crucial for operating your digital properties. Here are key considerations to navigate:

a. Jurisdictional Compliance: Understand the legal requirements specific to the jurisdictions in which your digital properties operate or target users. Familiarize yourself with local laws, regulations, and industry-specific compliance obligations to ensure adherence.

b. Advertising and Marketing Regulations: Comply with advertising and marketing regulations, including rules on disclosure, transparency, and fair competition. Adhere to guidelines from regulatory bodies such as the Federal Trade Commission (FTC) or Advertising Standards Authority (ASA) to avoid misleading or deceptive practices.

c. Accessibility Compliance: Ensure that your digital properties are accessible to individuals with disabilities, complying with accessibility standards such as the Web Content Accessibility Guidelines (WCAG). Consider providing alternative formats, assistive technologies, and accessible design elements to accommodate diverse user needs.

d. Financial and Legal Disclosures: Provide accurate and complete financial and legal disclosures on your digital properties. Adhere to regulations governing disclosures related to financial transactions, investments, affiliate relationships, or any other relevant legal obligations.

e. Monitoring Regulatory Updates: Stay up to date with evolving regulations and industry standards related to digital properties. Monitor changes in laws, policies, and guidelines to ensure ongoing compliance and make necessary adjustments to your operations when required.

Navigating legal and ethical considerations requires continuous vigilance and adherence to applicable laws and regulations. Stay informed about changes in intellectual property, privacy, and compliance landscapes, seek legal advice when needed, and adopt best practices to protect your digital properties and maintain ethical business practices.

8.1 Intellectual Property and Copyrights

Protecting intellectual property (IP) and respecting copyrights are essential for maintaining the legal integrity of your digital properties. Here's a closer look at key considerations:

Copyright Ownership: Understand the concept of copyright and ensure that you have the proper ownership or licensing rights for any content or creative works associated with your digital properties. Be aware of the copyright duration and expiration dates for different types of intellectual property.

Originality and Fair Use: Create original content for your digital properties to avoid infringing on the copyrights of others. Familiarize yourself with the concept of fair use, which allows for the limited use of copyrighted material without permission, but be mindful of its limitations and seek legal advice when in doubt.

Licensing and Permissions: Obtain necessary permissions or licenses for any copyrighted material you use in your digital properties, including images, music, videos, or written content. Ensure that you comply with the terms of the licenses and properly attribute the content to the original creators.

Trademarks and Branding: Protect your trademarks and branding elements associated with your digital properties. Conduct comprehensive trademark searches before adopting a new brand or domain name to avoid infringing on existing trademarks. Consider registering your trademarks to establish legal protection and enforce your rights.

DMCA Compliance: Familiarize yourself with the Digital Millennium Copyright Act (DMCA) and its provisions. If your digital properties allow user-generated content, implement procedures for responding to copyright infringement claims, including the process for taking down infringing material when notified.

Intellectual Property Audits: Periodically conduct intellectual property audits to ensure that you have proper ownership or licensing rights for all the content used in your digital properties. Regularly review your licenses and permissions to confirm their validity and compliance with copyright laws.

Protecting Your Intellectual Property: Take steps to protect your own intellectual property associated with your digital properties. Consider filing for copyright or trademark registration to establish legal rights and deter potential infringements. Implement measures to prevent unauthorized use or reproduction of your content.

Copyright Infringement Monitoring: Monitor your digital properties and online platforms to detect and address any instances of copyright infringement. Utilize online tools or services that can help identify unauthorized use of your copyrighted material and take appropriate actions to protect your rights.

Legal Assistance: Engage legal professionals who specialize in intellectual property law to provide guidance and assistance with copyright-related matters. They can help you navigate complex issues, respond to infringement claims, and take appropriate legal actions if necessary.

By understanding and adhering to intellectual property and copyright laws, you can protect your own intellectual property and respect the rights of others. Regularly review your intellectual property assets, secure proper licenses and permissions, and seek legal advice when needed. These measures will help ensure the legal integrity of your digital properties and safeguard your creative works in the digital realm.

8.2 Privacy and Data Protection

Protecting user privacy and ensuring data protection are crucial considerations for your digital properties. Here are more details on navigating privacy and data protection:

Data Collection and Consent:

Clearly disclose to users what personal data you collect, how it is used, and with whom it may be shared. Provide a transparent privacy policy that explains your data practices in plain language.

Obtain explicit and informed consent from users before collecting their personal data. Implement mechanisms such as checkboxes or consent banners to ensure users actively agree to your data collection and processing practices.

Data Security:

Implement robust security measures to safeguard user data from unauthorized access, breaches, or misuse. Use encryption, firewalls, secure storage, and other appropriate security technologies to protect personal data.

Regularly assess and update your security practices to address emerging threats. Conduct security audits, penetration testing, and vulnerability assessments to identify and mitigate potential risks.

Privacy Policies:

Develop comprehensive privacy policies that outline how user data is collected, used, stored, and shared. Clearly state the purposes for which data is collected and the lawful basis for processing it.

Make privacy policies easily accessible on your digital properties, typically through a dedicated privacy policy page or link in the website footer. Ensure that your policies are up to date, accurate, and reflect your current data practices.

Cookie Compliance:

Comply with cookie laws and regulations by providing transparent information about the use of cookies or similar tracking technologies on your digital properties.

Offer users clear options to manage their cookie preferences, including providing a cookie consent banner or pop-up that allows users to accept or decline the use of non-essential cookies.

Ensure that you obtain proper consent for any cookies that require user consent under applicable laws.

International Data Transfers:

If your digital properties involve international data transfers, comply with data protection regulations governing such transfers. For example, if you transfer data from the European Union to the United States, ensure compliance with frameworks such as the EU-US Privacy Shield or rely on other lawful data transfer mechanisms, like Standard Contractual Clauses (SCCs).

Conduct a data protection impact assessment (DPIA) to identify and address any potential risks associated with cross-border data transfers.

User Rights:

Respect and uphold the rights of users regarding their personal data. Be aware of individuals' rights, such as the right to access, rectify, erase, or restrict the processing of their data. Provide a process for users to exercise these rights.

Respond promptly and appropriately to user requests related to their data rights. Establish procedures for handling data subject access requests (DSARs) and ensure compliance with relevant data protection laws.

Data Retention:

Establish data retention policies that specify the duration for which you retain personal data. Ensure that your data retention practices align with legal requirements and the purposes for which the data was collected.

Regularly review and securely dispose of personal data that is no longer necessary or required to be retained. Implement processes to securely delete or anonymize data when it is no longer needed.

Compliance Audits and Assessments:

Conduct regular privacy and data protection audits to assess your compliance with applicable laws and regulations. Identify areas of improvement and take necessary actions to address any gaps or vulnerabilities.

Consider engaging independent third parties to conduct privacy assessments or obtain certifications that demonstrate your commitment to privacy and data protection.

Data Breach Response:

Establish an incident response plan to effectively handle and mitigate data breaches. Develop procedures for notifying affected individuals, regulatory authorities, and other stakeholders in the event of a data breach.

Train your staff on their responsibilities and roles in responding to data breaches, ensuring they are aware of the necessary steps to take to minimize harm and protect affected individuals.

Regulatory Updates:

Stay updated with evolving privacy and data protection regulations. Monitor changes in laws, regulations, industry standards, and best practices to ensure ongoing compliance with privacy requirements.

Regularly review and update your privacy practices, policies, and procedures to reflect changes in the legal and regulatory landscape.

Navigating privacy and data protection requires ongoing commitment to ensuring the security and privacy of user data. Implement strong data protection measures, maintain transparent data practices, and adhere to applicable laws and regulations to establish trust and protect user privacy within your digital properties.

8.3 Compliance and Regulations

Compliance with relevant laws and regulations is essential to ensure the legal and ethical operation of your digital properties. Here are more details on navigating compliance and regulations:

Jurisdictional Compliance:

Understand the legal requirements specific to the jurisdictions in which your digital properties operate or target users. Different countries or regions may have specific laws and regulations that apply to various aspects of your operations.

Conduct thorough research and consult legal professionals to ensure that you comply with local laws, including those related to data protection, consumer rights, advertising, intellectual property, and taxation.

Advertising and Marketing Regulations:

Comply with advertising and marketing regulations to ensure transparency, fairness, and ethical practices. Adhere to guidelines set by regulatory bodies, such as the Federal Trade Commission (FTC) in the United States or Advertising Standards Authority (ASA) in the United Kingdom.

Review and comply with rules regarding disclosure, endorsement, truthfulness, and fair competition. Avoid deceptive or misleading practices and ensure that advertising claims are accurate and substantiated.

Accessibility Compliance:

Ensure that your digital properties are accessible to individuals with disabilities. Familiarize yourself with accessibility standards such as the Web Content Accessibility Guidelines (WCAG) to provide an inclusive experience for all users.

Implement accessible design practices, provide alternative text for images, offer keyboard navigation options, and make sure that audio and video content are accompanied by captions or transcripts.

Financial and Legal Disclosures:

Provide accurate and complete financial and legal disclosures on your digital properties. Comply with applicable regulations regarding financial transactions, investments, affiliate relationships, or any other relevant legal obligations.

Clearly present terms of service, refund policies, pricing details, and any other information that users need to make informed decisions. Ensure that disclosures are prominently displayed and easily accessible.

Monitoring Regulatory Updates:

Stay informed about changes in laws, regulations, and industry standards relevant to your digital properties. Regularly review updates from regulatory authorities and industry organizations to ensure ongoing compliance.

Subscribe to newsletters, follow industry publications, and engage with legal professionals or consultants specialized in your industry to stay updated on the latest regulatory developments.

Compliance Audits and Assessments:

Conduct regular compliance audits to assess your adherence to applicable laws and regulations. Identify areas of non-compliance or potential risks and take appropriate actions to address them.

Engage legal professionals or compliance experts to perform audits or assessments, providing an objective evaluation of your compliance efforts.

Staff Training and Awareness:

Train your staff on relevant compliance requirements and legal obligations. Ensure that they are aware of their responsibilities and understand the implications of non-compliance.

Regularly update staff training to reflect changes in regulations, emerging risks, and best practices. Encourage a culture of compliance within your organization.

Regulatory Reporting and Documentation:

Maintain accurate records and documentation to demonstrate your compliance efforts. Keep track of policies, procedures, consent forms, contracts, and any other relevant documentation.

Establish processes for reporting and documenting incidents, breaches, or complaints. Document your response, actions taken, and any remedial measures implemented.

Legal Assistance:

Seek legal assistance from professionals with expertise in the relevant areas of law. Engage legal counsel or consultants who specialize in compliance and regulatory matters to provide guidance and support.

Consult legal professionals for advice on specific compliance requirements, interpretation of regulations, or navigating complex legal issues related to your digital properties.

By proactively navigating compliance and regulations, you can mitigate legal risks, establish trust with users and stakeholders, and ensure the ethical operation of your digital properties. Stay informed, conduct audits, train your staff, and seek legal advice when needed to maintain compliance and protect your organization's reputation.

Chapter 9: Future Trends and Emerging Technologies

9.1 The Impact of Artificial Intelligence and Automation

Artificial Intelligence (AI) and automation are revolutionizing the digital real estate industry. Here's a closer look at their impact:

a. Personalized User Experiences: AI-powered algorithms can analyze user data and preferences to deliver personalized content and recommendations, enhancing user engagement and satisfaction.

b. Chatbots and Virtual Assistants: Chatbots and virtual assistants powered by AI can handle customer inquiries, provide support, and streamline communication, improving efficiency and enhancing the user experience.

c. Property Search and Recommendations: AI algorithms can analyze vast amounts of data to help users find properties that match their preferences and requirements, simplifying the property search process and saving time for both buyers and renters.

d. Predictive Analytics: AI algorithms can analyze market trends, user behavior, and property data to provide predictive insights. This helps investors make informed decisions about property investments, pricing, and market trends.

e. Property Management Automation: AI and automation can streamline property management tasks, such as rent collection, maintenance scheduling, and tenant communication, improving operational efficiency and reducing human error.

9.2 Blockchain and Cryptocurrencies in Digital Real Estate

Blockchain technology and cryptocurrencies have the potential to transform the digital real estate industry. Consider the following:

a. Smart Contracts: Blockchain-based smart contracts can automate and enforce the terms of property transactions, ensuring transparency, security, and reducing the need for intermediaries.

b. Property Ownership and Title Records: Blockchain can provide secure and tamper-proof property ownership records, simplifying the transfer of property ownership and reducing the risk of fraud.

c. Fractional Ownership and Tokenization: Blockchain enables fractional ownership of real estate, allowing investors to purchase and trade fractional shares of properties. Tokenization of real estate assets provides liquidity and accessibility to a wider pool of investors.

d. Real Estate Crowdfunding: Blockchain and cryptocurrencies enable decentralized crowdfunding platforms, allowing investors to participate in real estate projects with lower investment thresholds, increased transparency, and reduced intermediaries.

e. Cross-Border Transactions: Cryptocurrencies can facilitate faster and more cost-effective cross-border transactions, eliminating the need for traditional banking systems and reducing transaction fees and settlement times.

9.3 Exploring the Metaverse: Virtual Reality and Augmented Reality

Virtual Reality (VR) and Augmented Reality (AR) are shaping the future of digital real estate. Consider the following:

a. Immersive Property Tours: VR technology allows users to experience virtual property tours, enabling remote buyers to explore properties in a realistic and immersive manner.

b. Virtual Staging: VR and AR can be used to virtually stage properties, showcasing different interior designs and configurations without physically furnishing the spaces.

c. Architectural Visualization: VR and AR can assist architects, developers, and buyers in visualizing and experiencing properties before they are built, improving design decisions and enhancing pre-construction marketing.

d. Virtual Collaboration and Remote Work: VR and AR technologies enable virtual collaboration, allowing remote teams to work together on real estate projects, conduct virtual meetings, and make informed decisions without the need for physical presence.

e. Integration with Metaverses: The emergence of metaverses, virtual worlds where users interact with each other and digital assets, opens up opportunities for virtual real estate ownership, virtual commerce, and social experiences within immersive digital environments.

As these technologies continue to advance, they have the potential to reshape the way we buy, sell, and interact with real estate in the digital realm. Keeping an eye on these future trends and emerging technologies can help you stay ahead of the curve and leverage new opportunities in the digital real estate landscape.

Chapter 10: Success Stories and Lessons from Digital Real Estate Entrepreneurs

10.1 Case Studies of Profitable Digital Property Investments

Examining successful digital property investments can provide valuable insights and lessons. Here are some case studies to consider:

a. Case Study 1: A digital entrepreneur identified an emerging niche market and purchased premium domain names related to that market. They developed websites with relevant content and attracted a significant audience. Leveraging targeted advertising and affiliate marketing, they generated substantial revenue through ad placements and commissions.

Key Lesson: Identifying untapped niche markets and acquiring premium domain names can be a lucrative strategy for building profitable digital properties.

b. Case Study 2: An investor recognized the growing popularity of video content and acquired a YouTube channel with a substantial subscriber base in a specific niche. By consistently uploading high-quality videos and monetizing the channel through sponsorships, brand partnerships, and advertising, they built a thriving digital property with a steady income stream.

Key Lesson: Acquiring established digital assets, such as popular social media accounts or YouTube channels, can provide a head start in building a successful online presence.

c. Case Study 3: An entrepreneur identified the potential of virtual real estate within a popular metaverse and invested in virtual land parcels early on. As the metaverse gained traction, the value of the virtual properties skyrocketed. They subsequently leased the virtual land to businesses and individuals, generating substantial rental income.

Key Lesson: Recognizing the potential of emerging digital platforms, such as metaverses, and investing in virtual real estate can offer significant returns on investment.

10.2 Interviews with Industry Experts and Thought Leaders

Engaging with industry experts and thought leaders can provide valuable insights and guidance. Here are some potential interview topics to explore:

a. Investment Strategies: Interview successful digital real estate entrepreneurs and experts to gain insights into their investment strategies. Discuss their approaches to identifying lucrative opportunities, diversifying portfolios, and mitigating risks.

b. Monetization Techniques: Speak with experts who have successfully monetized their digital properties. Explore their revenue generation strategies, including advertising, e-commerce, subscriptions, licensing, or innovative approaches specific to their niche.

c. Technology Adoption: Interview thought leaders who have embraced emerging technologies in the digital real estate space. Learn how they incorporate AI, blockchain, VR, or other cutting-edge technologies into their digital properties and the impact on their success.

d. Market Trends and Future Outlook: Engage industry experts to discuss current market trends and predictions for the future of digital real estate. Explore topics such as the evolution of virtual marketplaces, the impact of regulatory changes, or the potential of new technologies.

e. Lessons Learned and Advice: Seek the wisdom of experienced entrepreneurs who have navigated challenges and achieved success in the digital real estate industry. Gather their insights, lessons learned, and practical advice for aspiring digital real estate entrepreneurs.

By studying successful case studies and conducting interviews with industry experts and thought leaders, you can gain valuable knowledge, learn from their experiences, and apply their insights to your own digital real estate ventures. These stories and lessons provide inspiration, guidance, and a deeper understanding of the strategies that lead to success in the dynamic digital real estate landscape.

The rise of digital real estate has opened up a world of opportunities for entrepreneurs and investors alike. In this comprehensive guide, we explored the concept of digital real estate, its evolution, benefits, and the wide range of opportunities it offers. We delved into various types of digital properties, such as websites, domains, social media assets, and virtual real estate within metaverses.

To succeed in the digital real estate market, thorough research and evaluation are crucial. We discussed market analysis, assessing the potential value of online properties, and conducting due diligence and risk assessment. Monetization strategies were explored, including advertising, affiliate marketing, e-commerce, content creation, and virtual real estate rentals.

We also provided insights into strategies for acquiring digital properties, such as participating in auctions, leveraging marketplaces and brokers, and identifying profitable investment opportunities. Negotiating and closing deals requires skill and understanding of market dynamics.

Managing and optimizing digital properties involves website development, social media management, and virtual real estate maintenance and enhancement. We emphasized the importance of growing your digital real estate portfolio through diversification, risk management, scaling, and leveraging investments.

Navigating legal and ethical considerations is essential. We covered intellectual property and copyrights, privacy and data protection, as well as compliance and regulations. Understanding these areas ensures the legal integrity and ethical operation of your digital properties.

We then explored future trends and emerging technologies that are shaping the digital real estate landscape. Artificial intelligence and automation, blockchain and cryptocurrencies, and virtual reality and augmented reality offer exciting possibilities for innovation and growth.

Lastly, we highlighted success stories and lessons from digital real estate entrepreneurs, including case studies of profitable investments and the value of engaging with industry experts and thought leaders.

As the digital real estate frontier continues to evolve, it is essential to stay informed, adapt to emerging technologies, and embrace new opportunities. By leveraging the knowledge and strategies outlined in this guide, you can navigate the dynamic landscape of digital real estate, build a successful portfolio, and thrive in this exciting and ever-expanding market.

www.ingramcontent.com/pod-product-compliance
Lightning Source LLC
Chambersburg PA
CBHW021745150726
47989CB00004B/1527